D0188688

a smart girl's guide to her parents' divorce

how to land on your feet when your world turns upside down

by Nancy Holyoke
illustrated by Scott Nash

CALGARY PUBLIC LIBRARY

American Girl®

JUL - 2009

Published by American Girl Publishing, Inc.

Copyright © 2009 by American Girl, LLC

All rights reserved. No part of this book may be used or reproduced in any manner whatsoever without written permission except in the case of brief quotations embodied in critical articles and reviews.

Questions or comments? Call 1-800-845-0005,
visit our Web site at americangirl.com, or write to Customer Service,
American Girl, 8400 Fairway Place, Middleton, WI 53562.

Printed in China

09 10 11 12 13 LEO 10 9 8 7 6 5 4 3 2 1

All American Girl marks are trademarks of American Girl, LLC.

Editorial Development: Michelle Watkins, Judith Woodburn, Therese Maring
Art Direction and Design: Chris Lorette David
Production: Jeannette Bailey, Gretchen Krause, Julie Kimmell, Judith Lary
Consultant: Patricia K. Criswell, ACSW
Illustrations: Scott Nash

This book is not intended to replace the advice of psychologists or other health-care professionals. It should be considered an additional resource only. Questions and concerns about mental health should always be discussed with a health-care provider.

Dear Reader,

One out of every two marriages in America ends in divorce. That doesn't make it any easier for girls like you, but it does mean that there are lots of other kids around who have made the kind of changes you're facing now. If they could do it, you can, too. Here are a few things to keep in mind:

You won't feel like this forever

Divorce is a process. It's not over in a day or a week. It takes a long time. If your parents are in the middle of a divorce right now, you may be so upset you feel as if your head's on fire. But that doesn't mean you'll feel like this forever. Time helps. Emotions cool. Situations change.

You came from love

Divorce can't erase the past. Your parents may not love each other now, but they loved each other once. You came from that love, and it lives on in you.

Divorce doesn't predict the future, either. You aren't going to be divorced just because your parents divorced. Divorce doesn't determine who you are or what you can do in life.

Talk, talk, talk

Whether your parents split up last week or ten years ago, if something is on your mind, say so. Talk to your mom or dad. Talk to your brothers and sisters. Talk to an adult you trust—a favorite cousin, your Aunt Sue, your best friend's mom. Talk to your teacher or a counselor at school.

Talking makes you feel better—simple as that. It relieves bad feelings. It helps you figure out what you think. It helps you make good decisions. And that, of course, is what we hope this book will do, too.

Your friends at American Girl

contents

splitting up

Your parents' separation may be one of the hardest things you'll ever face. You could well have a storm of feelings in your chest—shock, fear, relief, anger, sadness. When that storm blows hardest, remember that divorce may mean the end of your parents' marriage, but *it's not the end of your family.* The family is changing, but the family's going on. And you will, too.

how could this happen?

My parents are getting divorced. Whenever I even think about it, I get so upset. I never thought that this would ever happen.

Very Upset

People change over the years, and their feelings about each other may change, too. Sometimes a couple grow closer together. Sometimes they grow further apart. It's not easy to say how that happens.

Growing apart

Think about your own friendships. Who were your best friends in first grade? Are they still your best friends? Maybe some are. But some probably aren't. Chances are you didn't have a big fight. You just got interested in different things. You became different sorts of people.

Something similar can happen with marriage. Two people who were once very close may find over time that they disagree about some very basic things in life—about money and jobs, about family and friends, about what's important to them and what makes them happy.

Fights that don't stop

They may also fight.

Not all fights are bad. A lot of happy couples fight and feel better afterward because they've expressed their differences and found ways to compromise. But when a couple can't find ways to agree or to make up, there's trouble. They stop listening to each other. They stop caring about each other's feelings. The fight never stops. Anger burns through the relationship till little's left. The day may come when one or both of these people decide the marriage can't be fixed.

By then, most parents have been worrying for a long time about how their problems with each other are affecting their kids. They know their children want them together. They also know that deeply unhappy adults create an unhappy home. They try to think about the future, as well as about today. They divorce when they're convinced that the family has a better chance of happiness if the two of them live apart. It's not an easy choice, but they've come to believe it's the best one.

scared

Please help me. My parents are getting a divorce. They have been married for 13 years. I love them both, and I want to be with both of them. I am so-o-o-o scared.

Scared

It's true that when your parents are living in two homes you can't be with them both at the same time. That will take some getting used to. But don't assume that you're going to lose one of your parents. Your ties to each of them are as strong today as they ever were. *Your parents love you.* The fact that they're going to be living in separate homes does nothing—*nothing*—to change that. Your parents are divorcing each other. They're not divorcing you.

Speak up

So talk to your mom and dad. Ask what decisions have been made about where you'll live and how often you'll see them both. Tell them what you want, too (write it down beforehand if that's easier). Ask your parents for a calendar and have them help you fill in the days you'll be with each of them in the coming month. Seeing everything written out will help you picture just how all of this will work.

Ask for reassurance

Having your parents in two different homes will seem strange at first. But your mom and dad are perfectly capable of running their own homes and living independently. If you ever doubt that, let them know: "I'm scared. Are we going to be O.K.?" Give them a chance to say "Yes, we'll be fine," and as the days pass you'll begin to see it's true.

advice from girls

Parents are for keeps

The one thought that gave me comfort was "Mom will still be my mom and Dad will still be my dad." The divorce can't change that.

Feeling Better

guilt

> **My parents are getting divorced. I feel like it's all my fault. I feel I should get blamed for it. I'm too ashamed to say anything.**
>
> FEELING GUILTY

No way is this divorce your fault.

It doesn't matter what you did or didn't do. It doesn't matter what you said or didn't say. It doesn't matter if your parents fought about you. It doesn't even matter if other people blame you: they're wrong.

Kids don't cause divorces

Parents disagree about their kids in happy marriages, too. The real problem is that your parents' relationship has broken down. This has to do with their choices and actions—not yours. You didn't cause the breakdown. And you sure couldn't have fixed it.

So why all this guilt?

You may know you're not at fault but still feel a twinge of guilt. Why's that? For the same reason you may think your favorite baseball team wins when you watch the game and loses when you don't. People are superstitious. We tend to think our own actions make a difference even when they don't.

Don't keep quiet about guilty feelings. Talk to your parents and let them set you straight. Then say this in your mind till you believe it: a child is never responsible for her parents' divorce—*ever.*

’s not my fault.
s not my fault.
’s not my fault.

mixed emotions

My brother doesn't seem to care that my dad's gone, but my sister cries constantly. I'm like in between. Sometimes I cry and sometimes I don't care. Is that O.K.?

Sad and Glad

Absolutely. There is no "right" way to feel about a divorce.

When one parent leaves, it can be a relief. That's especially true when there's been a lot of fighting. Everyone is more relaxed. You can breathe again. You may feel happy for the first time in months.

Tears are O.K.

At the same time, the end of a marriage is almost always very sad. In some ways, a divorce is like a death. Your parents' marriage was precious to you. Crying is not only O.K., it's a necessary part of the grieving process. If you try to act cheery because you think your mom or dad wants you to be cheery, the tears might get bottled up inside you for years.

A divorce can also leave you feeling numb. Sometimes a girl can have so many emotions in a day that her mind and heart simply have to take a rest, and shut down for a while. As long as they don't stay shut down, that's O.K., too.

Glad and sad?

It sounds as if you feel relieved, sad, *and* numb. Does that mean you're confused? No. It means you're working through all your feelings to understand and accept the divorce. Just keep talking to your parents. Stay involved with your friends and activities. Trust yourself. And don't be afraid to say what you think. It will make you feel better. You'll also be setting a good example for your brother, who surely feels more than he shows.

advice from girls

Let it out

When my parents first split up, I held all of my feelings inside. It made me feel really sick. But after I talked to my cousin and one of my best friends, I felt a lot better. So my advice is talk to someone who understands. Let it out. Don't hold it all in.

Relieved

feeling angry

My parents are getting separated. I've been having fights with my friends because I am so angry and sad. I don't know how to get through it.

Mixed Up and Mad

A lot of anger comes from feeling hurt. It's hard to understand how your parents could do something that upsets you this much. You may think: *I trusted them, and now they're ruining my life! If they loved me, they would see how this is killing me and stop!* As the thoughts grow in your mind, sadness and anger rise in your throat.

It's O.K. to be angry. And you should tell your parents just how mad you are. Being able to talk about these feelings gets them out of your system so that, little by little, the fury will die out. Until then, here are some things you can do.

Explain

Tell your friends you're going through a hard time. Ask them to let you know if you've said something hurtful. Be ready to apologize when you have. It may be smart to avoid people and situations you know might irritate you.

Write it out

Turn your anger into words. Write a letter you'll never send or start an anger journal, where you can blow your stack. In every entry ask yourself: What am I mad about? Why does it make me mad? What can I do about it?

Talk it over

Talk to your brother or sister, your grandma or a good friend. A sympathetic listener will calm you down and help you find words for how you feel. Afterward you'll be able to express yourself better with your mom and dad.

Blow off steam

Give your muscles something to do. It will distract you and cool you down. If you're only a little mad, go for a walk, play with the dog, or clean your room. If you're furious, go for a run and pound your anger into the ground with every step. Slam a tennis ball. Punch a pillow. Keep going till you're sweaty and drained of energy. You'll be drained of the worst part of your anger, too.

upset parents

My mom is always crying. My dad is always yelling. Before the divorce they did not yell or cry. Now I'm scared of them!

Scared of My Parents

Tell your mom and dad how you feel as plainly as you can: "I miss how it used to be! You didn't cry and yell like this before the divorce. It scares me. I don't know what to do. Please stop." Right now, your parents are so caught up in their own feelings that they aren't thinking about how their behavior is affecting you. They need a reminder, and you're perfectly right to give it to them.

Cooler company

Talking to another adult can also be a big help. Is there an aunt you trust and like? A counselor at school? A family friend or neighbor? Divorce is a process that takes time. Your parents are still in the middle of it. They'll calm down eventually and become more like themselves again. Until then, an adult with a cool head and a warm heart may be just what you need.

taking sides

I hate to say this, but my mom and dad are splitting apart! I think I should stand up with my mom and drop my dad. I still love him. It's just that I don't like him.
Do not know what to do!

1. You do *not* have to take sides. Don't let anybody tell you that you do. *This is not your divorce; this is not your fight.* You don't have to get angry with your dad to stay loyal to your mom.

2. Be careful about deciding one parent is the bad guy. Most of the time the split comes as a result of problems both people have contributed to.

3. Your dad's clearly done something you don't like, and you want to support your mom. That's fine. But if you "drop" the dad you love, you'll miss him. Sooner or later, you may regret dropping him. You'll feel sad and get angry, and that anger will come out at your mom—or even at yourself.

You may not like your dad right now, but he's still your dad. Let him know where you stand. If you're not ready to do something he wants you to do, say so. If you think he's behaving badly, tell him that. Be honest. Tell him what you think and how you feel. Write him a letter if that's easier. Just don't feel guilty about loving him. And don't lock him out of your life.

told nothing

My dad moved out over the summer. I feel confused. I try to ask people what I am concerned about, but no one gives me a straight answer.

Need Some Answers

Your parents are making a common mistake: not talking to their children.

They may be afraid that discussing their separation will upset you. They may be afraid that they'll get upset themselves. Their own plans and feelings may be such a jumble that they don't know what to say. Or they may want to keep some issues private.

Your parents *do* have a right to privacy, and some topics will be off-limits. At the same time, you have a right to ask for help in understanding what's going on. "Are you getting divorced? Where will I live? Who will take care of me? When will I get to see you? Will we have to move?" Questions like these, about your future and daily life, are perfectly O.K.

Try again

So try this. Pick a good moment, approach your parents one at a time, and say flat out: "I respect your privacy, but I deserve to know what's going on. Your silence is confusing me." Speak calmly and firmly. Ask them to turn off the TV or put down the newspaper. If Mom still won't talk, try your dad. If Dad won't talk, either, you might go to your grandparents or other relatives for help. You might also write a letter to your mom and dad, listing all the questions you have. They may be surprised at what they read.

Silence = misunderstandings

Maybe they thought you knew Dad had an apartment—but you didn't. Maybe you've been worrying that you'll have to move—but you won't.

A parent who tells a child nothing leaves her to wonder and worry in the dark. You're right to get those questions out in the open. Your parents would be right to answer them.

quiz

can you speak your mind?

Parents aren't the only ones who have trouble talking about divorce. How good are you at saying what you think? Circle your answers.

1. Your dad moved out three weeks ago. Today Mom says, "You look sad. Want to talk about it?"

   a. You say, "I had a bad day." If you mention Dad, Mom might start crying.

   b. You walk off. Mom wants you to tell her how you feel? Fat chance—she's the one who wants the divorce!

   c. "No, thanks," you say, smiling. "I'm fine."

   d. You say, "Yes," and tell her what you're thinking.

2. Last month, your dad left your mom for Sonya. Now he wants you to meet her.

   a. You say, "I'm really busy this week."

   b. You say, "I hate her, and I'll always hate her. And I hate you, too."

   c. "O.K.," you say—and think you're going to be sick.

   d. You say, "No. I'm too angry about what you did. I'm not ready yet."

3. One question has been gnawing at you all week: are you going to have to move? Now here comes Mom to say good night.

   a. You say, "I love my room."

   b. You say, "What terrible thing are you going to do to me next?"

   c. You just smile and hug her. If you're very sweet and helpful, maybe she won't let the move happen.

   d. You say, "Mom, are we going to move?"

4. When Mom picks you up at Dad's, the two of them get into a big fight. Afterward, Mom says, "What a jerk. Aren't you glad to be coming home?"
   a. You say nothing.
   b. You yell, "You're wrecking my whole life! You only think about yourself."
   c. You say, "Yes." But when you get to your mom's, you go up to your room and cry.
   d. You say, "Don't ask me to take sides in your fights. It's wrong. And please don't call Dad names in front of me."

answers

The Dodger

If you circled mostly a's, you avoid tough subjects. You're afraid your questions will upset people. You drop hints and hope your parents will figure out what you want. Does this work? Sadly, no. Don't make life a guessing game. Take off the gag and let yourself talk.

The Attacker

If you circled mostly b's, your anger makes you blow up, clam up, or walk out. You may have good reasons to be angry, but you'll never get your parents to understand a problem if you can't discuss it. Don't attack and accuse. Try starting sentences with "I feel . . ." or "I think . . ." instead.

The Actor

If you circled mostly c's, you pretend things are O.K. when they're not. Maybe you hope that being cheerful and good will prevent bad things from happening. All it really does is confuse your parents. When you say nothing is bothering you, they will think you're fine when you're not. Don't play a role. Be yourself.

The Straight-Shooter

If you circled mostly d's, you do a good job of saying how you feel and what you want. You won't walk away from every conversation happy, but that's O.K. Sometimes you'll upset people—that's O.K., too. You're being true to yourself. And you're talking openly, with trust and respect, to the people you love. And *that* will get you through most anything.

custody

My mom and dad are fighting over me and who I should live with. I want to live with my mom, but my dad doesn't want me to. Am I old enough to decide who I should live with?

Old Enough?

No. The decision about where you will live has to be made by an adult.

Usually, a child's parents decide. If the parents can't agree, then they will go to court and a judge will make the decision for them. Most judges try to find a way to help the child stay close to both parents. Custody arrangements are never carved in stone. They can always change—and often do—as the situation changes.

Your wishes

You can and should talk with your mom and dad about what you want and why. If your case goes to court, you may also have a chance to express your opinion to a person assigned by the judge to interview you.

How much weight a judge gives a girl's wishes depends on her age. It also depends on why she wants what she wants. If you want to live with your mom because you feel close to her and because she's always taken care of you, those are great reasons. If you want to live with her because you feel sorry for her or because she has a wide-screen TV, those are poor ones.

Other factors

Whatever your reasoning, your wishes aren't the only thing your parents or a judge will consider. They will also ask themselves questions like these:

- What decision gives you and your brothers and sisters the fewest changes to deal with?
- Has one parent provided most of the daily child care in the past? That is, has one parent cooked the meals, drawn the baths, helped with homework, and been involved at school?
- What sort of child care can each parent give to your little sister?
- And what sort of after-school supervision can they provide for you?
- Are there family and friends nearby at your mom's? At your dad's?
- Are both your parents healthy and responsible?

The big question

What this all boils down to is: what's best for the children?

It's a big question—bigger than any one person in the family. What you want is important. But what you need to grow and flourish is more important yet.

how divorce works

> **I have a bad problem. My parents are getting divorced. I don't know what it is like or how it works. Help me!**
>
> Clueless

Everybody knows what it means to *be* divorced. But, like you, most people don't know exactly how a couple *get* divorced until they've been closely involved with a divorce themselves. The process is different in every state and for every family. But here's help with some of the new words you may be hearing around the house.

Separation

When two married people stop living together, they are *separated.* A separation is usually a temporary situation. Separations often end when the marriage is legally dissolved in divorce.

Divorce

Divorce is a legal action two people take to end their marriage. The laws that spell out how they have to do this are sometimes complicated, but they protect people in all sorts of ways.

Usually, a lot of time passes between the time the couple decide they want to divorce and the day the divorce is final.

Separation agreement

Two people have to make a lot of decisions when they divorce. How will they divide their money? Who will pay old bills? Most important, how will they share responsibilities for their children?

Often parents will hire lawyers and a mediator to help them agree on all these questions. When decisions are made, they get written up in a *separation agreement,* which both parents sign and a judge approves.

Mediator

Mediators are trained to help divorcing couples sit down together and make agreements. They can help people resolve differences.

Lawyer

Typically, each parent has a *lawyer* during a divorce. The lawyer's job is to negotiate for the parent and help him or her get the best agreement possible on issues like custody and child support. Generally, both sides have to compromise.

Custody

Custody has to do with the right to take care of a child. There are two basic issues in custody:

- Where will you live? How much time will you spend with each parent and when? This kind of custody is sometimes called *physical custody.*
- Who will make the big decisions about your life? *Big* decisions. That means things like where you go to school and what doctor you see—not what TV shows you can watch or when you have to go to bed. This kind of custody is sometimes called *legal custody.*

These two kinds of custody can be shared by your parents in various ways. Custody can also be the responsibility of one parent only. (In special cases, custody is given to another relative or a foster parent, but this is unusual.)

The words people use to talk about the various ways of dividing custody differ from state to state. If you want to know what a term like "joint custody" means in your town, ask one of your parents or a counselor.

Child support

Child support is the money parents pay to help take care of their children. The parent you live with most of the time will probably receive child support from your other parent to help pay for things you need (your food and clothes, and so on).

Judge

If a divorcing couple can't come to an agreement on custody, child support, and other issues, then their lawyers argue their differences in a special court. If your parents go to court, it doesn't mean they've done anything wrong. It just means they need help deciding their differences.

A *judge* will hear both sides and then make the decision for them.

If a couple continue to disagree about raising the children after the divorce is final, they may go back to court again.

The judge's job is always the same: to make a fair decision.

Guardian ad litem, court counselor, and evaluator

If your parents go to court, the judge may appoint someone to interview you to find out what you want. This person might be called a *court counselor*, an *evaluator*, or a *guardian ad litem* (add LIGHT-um). He or she studies your family and tells the judge what would be best for you and your brothers and sisters.

If you talk with someone like this, be honest about what you feel and what you want. This is your chance to speak up. Think about what's good for *you*—not what you think might be good for your parents.

Therapist or counselor

Therapists or *counselors* help adults and kids deal with the complicated feelings that may come with divorce. They are not part of the legal process.

counseling

My parents are divorced. I need someone to talk to besides my parents, but I don't know who.

Wondering

A therapist's office is a safe place where you can say what you think without worrying that someone will be hurt or upset. A therapist won't take sides with either parent. Instead, she or he will try to help you understand what's bothering you and what you can do to be happier. This person may also be able to express your point of view to your parents in a way you haven't been able to do yourself.

There are different kinds of counseling. In regular counseling, you talk to the therapist alone. In family counseling, the whole family goes and talks over problems together. In support groups, a bunch of kids gather with the therapist and share experiences.

Finding a counselor

To start, ask your parents if you can see a counselor. If they say O.K., they may ask friends or people at school to recommend someone who will be a good match for you. They can also make the appointment and get you to the office. Counseling with a private therapist costs money, but sometimes a parent's insurance will pay for it.

If your parents say that they don't want you to see a private therapist (or they can't afford to pay for one), then you should talk to a counselor at school. A school counselor is free. There might even be a support group at school for kids whose parents are divorced.

Religious organizations also often have counseling services. A priest, minister, rabbi, or mullah might be able to help you find someone, too.

The first time you go to a therapist, you may feel nervous. That's O.K. Start out by asking some questions: "Will you keep what I say a secret? How many times will I see you? What am I supposed to say and do?" The more you talk, the more natural it will feel.

Counseling can't solve your problems for you. It can help you understand what you really feel and think so that you are better able to solve those problems yourself.

advice from girls

"Ew, shrinks"

Although some kids go, "Ew, shrinks," it really helps to go to a therapist and talk it out. It helps to let out a lot of pent-up anger and hurt.

A Girl Who Got Help

telling your friends

My parents are divorcing. I am not quite sure how to tell my friends.

Embarrassed

A lot of kids worry during a divorce about how other people will react. They think: *My family is so messed up! No one else has these awful problems. We're not a normal family anymore.*

Not shameful

Not so. First off, every family has its problems, whether you see them or not. That's just a part of life. It's not shameful, and acting as if it were, by not talking about it, will only make you feel worse.

Second, every year about one million kids in this country see their parents divorce. That doesn't mean it's a great thing, but it does mean the kids at your school are used to it. You probably know girls whose parents aren't together. You don't think any less of them for that. Why should they think less of you?

Tell friends one at a time

Start with a girl you're especially close to. Pick a private time and place (say, after school at her house). Keep it simple—you don't need lots of details. If you need to cry, do. Tell a couple of other friends individually, too. As the circle of people who know gets wider, you'll find it easier to talk about the changes in your life.

You may find special comfort in talking to other girls whose parents are divorced. That's great. But hold on to old friends, too. A girl who hasn't experienced divorce herself can still care about you a lot. What you shared before, you share still.

advice from girls

That's O.K.

If your parents are divorced, that's O.K. It doesn't mean something is wrong with you or your parents.

Been There

moving

I am moving with my mom, sister, two cats, and hermit crabs, and maybe my dog and rabbits. I am sad and confused. I don't want to go far from everything, and plus I've never moved before!

Want to stay

Having to move during a divorce can make a girl feel as if she's losing everything she has. You *will* feel sad on and off—it's only natural. But in time, you'll set down roots like a plant in a fresh pot. One morning you'll wake up in this new place, feel that old warmth coming up from your toes, and think, *I'm O.K., I'm home.* Here are some ways to hurry that process.

Treasures

The week before you move, pack a special box with your most treasured things. Open it your first day in the new home. Be sure to include your favorite book so that you can curl up with it that night.

Room

Go to the library and check out some books that give you tips on fixing up a room. Spend the first few days in the new house making this the best room you've ever had.

Pets

Think about how to make the move nice for your cats and the hermit crabs. Do it.

Scrapbook

Make a scrapbook of your life. Include pictures from the time you were a baby up till today. As you meet new friends and do new things, keep adding photos. The more you add, the more you'll see that this move is not the end of everything. It's one more stop in the journey of your life.

Write

Keep in touch with people you love. Write a letter or an e-mail to your dad. While you're at it, write a letter or an e-mail to your best friend, too.

List

Make a list of all the things in your life that aren't changing. Put it where you'll see it every day.

Explore

Don't wait for your new neighborhood to discover you. Go discover it. Check out new places. Join a club or two. Your future's just beyond the door. March out and see what you can make of it.

wishful thinking

Many girls have wished that their parents would get back together. Many have imagined how that wish might come true. Some girls replay the fantasies in their mind like a movie with a happy ending. It's a way of escaping painful feelings. As long as the movie stops after a few minutes, it's O.K.

It's not O.K., though, if fantasies become so powerful that a girl begins to believe them. And it's not O.K. when a girl is constantly thinking about her parents' getting back together years after a divorce.

wishing

> My parents got divorced when I was four. Now I'm nine, and both are remarried. Every night I look up at the stars and wish they were together.
>
> Stargazer

When you want something *so* much, the wish feels almost magical. It seems that if only you cling to it, somehow, *some way,* that wish will come true.

But it won't. You know your parents aren't ever going to be a couple again. They've married other people and found happiness in other ways. You're stuck in the past with these lonely, hopeless feelings.

Break the spell

So try this: First, tell your mom and dad about your nighttime thoughts. Give them a chance to tell you how they feel about the divorce and their new partners. It'll bring you back to real life and help break the grip of secret fantasies. And that's good.

Focus on real life

Second, ask yourself if something else is bothering you—about your relationships with your parents and stepparents, or about friends or school. If so, talk it over with your parents and look for solutions. Solving a problem or two in the real world may make you less interested in the perfect world that exists only in your mind.

Finally, take charge of your thoughts at bedtime. Don't look at the stars and give yourself over to your wishes. Sing a song, talk to your stuffed pig, think about the book you read before lights-out. Do anything you can think of to turn your thoughts to other things, and keep at it. Sooner or later, that will help.

Most girls find that the wish to see their parents reunited never disappears entirely. Years from now, you may still be jolted by little fantasies that flash across your heart. That's fine. Just make sure you're in charge of your fantasies, and they're not in charge of you.

advice from girls

Fooling yourself

It's nice to dream that all you have to do is set up an unexpected meeting and your parents will forget about the divorce. On TV, sure, but not in real life. Don't try to fool yourself. Try to learn to live with it.

Keeping It Real

meddling

My parents are divorced, and I don't like it at all. It's all because of my dad. How can I get him to love my mom again?

So Sad

You can't.

Thinking you can trick your parents into getting remarried is one of the most common fantasies there is. But it's also one of the most dangerous, because a girl who thinks it's possible may do all sorts of crazy things. She may flunk a test or get into a fight or make herself sick in the hope that when her parents come together to deal with the problem, they'll end up falling in love again. Yet all that really happens is that she starts messing up her own life.

The truth is, nobody can make anybody love anybody else. That's just not how love works. You had nothing to do with your father's falling in love with your mother in the first place. You had nothing to do with that love's ending. And there is nothing you (or probably even your mom) can do to bring that love back.

Believe him

The decision to divorce is one of the most serious an adult will ever make. Ask your dad again if his decision is final. When he says yes, believe him.

advice from girls

Imagination

It's O.K. to think about the good times you and your mom and dad had together in the past, but don't let your imagination run wild about the future. Just enjoy the time you have with them now.

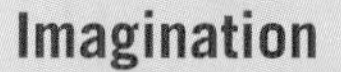

quiz

how big are your fantasies?

Have you ever had thoughts like these?
Put a check by your answers.

1. You're knocked to the ground in a soccer game. You aren't hurt, but you act as if you were. Maybe your mom and dad will both run over to help. They'll talk and decide they still love each other.

❑ Yes
❑ Maybe sometimes
❑ No

2. You pick another fight with your mom's boyfriend. You hate him, and you're going to be sure he hates you. Then he won't want to marry your mom, and she'll *have* to go back to your dad.

❑ Yes
❑ Maybe sometimes
❑ No

3. For the first time in months, your parents have a friendly conversation. You are so happy! Next week maybe they'll kiss each other!

❑ Yes
❑ Maybe sometimes
❑ No

4. Mom wants to get back together with Dad. All you need to do is persuade Dad to do it, and this whole miserable divorce will go away.

- ❑ Yes
- ❑ Maybe sometimes
- ❑ No

5. You refuse to fix up your new room at Dad's. Sooner or later, he'll be moving back in with you and Mom.

- ❑ Yes
- ❑ Maybe sometimes
- ❑ No

answers

Clear-eyed

If you mostly checked "no," you may not like this divorce, but you've accepted it. That frees you to get on with life and enjoy yourself.

Dreamy dreams

If you mostly checked "maybe sometimes," you know your parents won't remarry, but you can't quite say good-bye to old wishes. The sooner you do, the happier you'll be.

Get real

If you mostly checked "yes," wishful thinking is gumming up your life. You should be having fun—playing soccer, fixing up your room—not hatching plots and arguing with your mom's boyfriend.

The truth is, fantasies are just that—fantasies. In your heart, you know they won't come true. The more time you spend on them, the more time you spend feeling hopeless.

one girl,

two homes

Now Mom has her home and Dad has his. You may move between these places once a week. You may move between them once a month or once a year. In any case, the question you may ask yourself is "Which home is really mine?"

The answer depends a lot on the attitude you take with you when you go.

soccer ball

My parents are separated. They live far apart. I feel like a soccer ball, only instead of a field, it's the state of Minnesota.

Mad, sad, and confused

You're not alone. Lots of girls say they feel like an object that their parents are fighting over or trading back and forth. They're angry about the divorce and resentful that daily life is so complicated. Mad, sad, confused—you've got a right to have all these feelings, and to express them.

At the same time, going back and forth between your parents is now a fact of life. Sooner or later, you have to make a choice. You can curl up with your anger and see yourself as the ball getting kicked around. Or you can say, "I'm a person, not a thing, and I'm going to do something to help myself."

Make a nest

To be happy, you need to feel at home in both places.

At least one of your parents may be living in a house or apartment that's new to you. If you come and go as you would at a motel, without leaving a trace you were ever there, this place is never going to feel right.

So make your room your own. Decorate it. Work with your sister or stepsister if you share the space. Think of yourself as a bird building a nest. Every time you come, add a new twig. Whether it's a new poster or a box to hold your earrings, each improvement will give you pride and pleasure in this new place.

You should also keep some of your stuff in both homes. Knowing you're coming back to a favorite book or an old stuffed animal will make you feel a little happier every time you walk in the door.

Enjoy what's special

Maybe you've got friends and more familiar routines at Mom's, but at Dad's you have a dog and a great neighborhood to roam around in. For a lot of girls, having a variety of experiences and more stuff to do is one of the nice things about living in two homes.

Give it time

Finally, tell yourself that this is going to get easier as the months pass. You may never love the drive, but you'll notice it less as it becomes routine. For most families, divorce is a period of strong emotions and big changes. As life settles down, you'll discover that you're simply a girl with two loving parents and two loving homes—and that you truly do belong in both places.

missing Dad—and Mom

I only get to see my dad every two weeks for two days. I miss my dad a lot. But when I'm with my dad, I miss my mom a lot.

Without Them

There are lots of little things your parents do that have always been part of your day. Maybe your dad talks to the cat in the morning. Maybe your mom kisses you on both cheeks when you go to bed at night. It's moments like these that you miss most when you're apart. Each hole in your day is a heartache.

New routines

One thing that may help is coming up with new routines to fill some of those holes. If mornings are particularly sad, ask Mom if you can have Wacko Waffle Breakfasts once a week, where you both think up goofy ways to eat toaster waffles. If evenings are a problem, ask Dad if you two can read together before you go to bed. New routines can be bright spots in your week and take your mind off lonely thoughts.

The other big solution is, of course, to keep in touch, especially with the parent you don't get to see as often. There are lots of ways to do this.

Talk

Ask your dad if you two can set regular times to talk on the phone several times a week—say, Sundays at five, and Tuesdays and Thursdays at seven. It feels great to have something to plan for and look forward to.

Send messages

There are a lot of ways to send messages, and they're all fun: e-mails, text messages, voicemail, postcards, letters. You don't need to have any news. Even "Hey, Dad. I love you" is fine. And it will make you happy to get an "I love you, too" in return.

Share your life

Keep your parents up to date by saving and sharing schoolwork. Trade pictures and video clips, too. Dad might enjoy seeing Tuesday's soccer scrimmage, and Mom would get a kick out of that goat eating your corndog at the county fair.

Trade tokens

Special objects can remind you of people you love. Trade friendship bracelets with your mom. Ask your dad to pick up a seashell for you when he's at the beach. Mementos like these help you realize that no matter where you are and who you're with, you're always in your parents' hearts.

disorganized

My parents are divorced. Every time I go to my dad's house, I have to pack a bag with all my stuff. I am so unorganized!

Unorganized

To be organized, you need to be prepared. So here's what you do:

Check in

Make a checklist of things you usually need at your dad's. Take it to a local copy shop to be laminated (covered in plastic) so it can't get wet or torn. Make copies for both your parents, too. Punch a hole in the top of your list and attach it to your bag or backpack. Check it as you pack.

Use a calendar

Ask both parents to keep a monthly calendar in plain view that shows where you'll be every day of every week. Look at it often so that you can plan ahead.

Get two?

You can't have two of everything, but two toothbrushes, two combs, and a few extra pairs of socks and underwear can make life a lot easier. If you're always short of scrunchies or T-shirts, put them on the wish list for your next birthday.

Grab and go

Have a grab-and-go bin at both your mom's and your dad's. Always, always keep the things that travel back and forth with you in the bin. That way, when it's time to leave, you can just head for the bin, pull out your stuff, and toss it in your bag.

Check out

Time to leave? Stop! Look back at your checklist. Have you packed everything you brought? What's happening in the next few days? Should you bring anything else with you? A bit of thought now can save hours of fuss and bother later.

different rules

Whenever I am at my dad's house, he never lets me stay up late. He makes me go to bed before I'm tired.

Night Owl

Different homes have different rules. If the rules in Mom's house and Dad's house are so *very* different that it's confusing, you can ask your parents to get together and be more consistent. But generally speaking, you simply have to go along with the parent you're with.

Negotiate

That doesn't mean you can't discuss rules you dislike, just as you did before the divorce. It can be hard to fall asleep at nine if your mom lets you stay up till ten. Tell your dad that. Ask if he can live with a nine-thirty bedtime instead. Or if you want to stay up late-late on a weekend night, talk to him in a reasonable way about why you think it's O.K.

Make your case, then stop. If you keep going, you're nagging. Chances are, he'll be firm on some things, but on others he might be flexible.

Be patient

Even if your bedtime stays the same for now, your dad may think about what you've said. Sometimes parents try new rules in a new home and then find out that they don't really work. Your dad might switch bedtime to nine-thirty all on his own in a couple of months, when he sees for himself that you're lying awake in bed.

advice from girls

Different views

Your parents set different rules because they have different views on things. That's probably one of the reasons they divorced. You just have to deal with it. I've found I actually like things being different at each place.

Satisfied

busy mom

My mom is single and is very busy at her office. It is always around seven when she gets home. I miss her a lot. I really want my mom back.

Missing Mom

You can't change your mom's work hours. You *can* make the most of the hours you've got.

Do as much of your homework as you can before she gets home. Do any practicing you might have, too. That way, when your mom walks in the door you can spend the rest of the evening with her.

Pitch in

Chances are, your mom is just as busy after work as she is during the day. She may have to shop for food, stop at the cleaners, cook dinner, do laundry, help your brother with his homework, and see that the house is picked up. The best way to get more time with her is to help out.

Maybe you can make the salad while she makes the burgers. Maybe you can help fold laundry or put it away. It will give you time to talk, and it might even free her up to read a book with you or play a game of cards.

Save special time

You should also come right out and tell your mom that you miss spending time with her. Ask if you can call her after school every day at a certain time, just to check in. Suggest that the two of you set aside an hour or two every week when you drop everything and just have fun together. Maybe it's Friday-night movies and a bowl of popcorn. Maybe it's skating at the rink on Thursday after dinner or Sunday-morning bagels at the corner deli.

A lot of girls say that divorce helped them get to know their parents better. They shared more of their thoughts and feelings. They learned not to take each other for granted. It could be that pulling together through each hectic day will actually bring you and your mom closer, too.

advice from girls

Messages

My mom and I like to leave notes for each other. We say "Hi" or "Just wanted to check in" or "I just want to say I love you."

Writer

ignored

My parents are divorced. My dad is a doctor. All his free time is spent working on his house or on his computer. I try hard to be as important to him as these things. I've tried talking to him. Nothing works.

Heartbroken

You're a wise girl. You're thinking seriously about how to change this bad situation. Some girls get so angry and frustrated with a parent like this that they get into all sorts of trouble just to get attention. But that, of course, only makes everything worse.

Invitations

Invitations often work better than complaints. Pick a time when your dad's not already involved in a project or at the computer. Mealtime might be good. Don't say, "You never do anything with me." Instead, suggest specific activities the two of you can do together. For instance, "I need to work on my batting. Will you pitch to me after dinner?" Or "I really want to see that new movie. Want to go together tonight?" If he says yes—great.

If he says no, write the word on a piece of paper. Once you've collected five "no"s, bring them to your dad and put them in his lap. Say, "Dad, you turned me down five times. What would *you* like to do that we can do together? I'll say yes."

Another adult

You might also look for another adult to help you. Is there a step-mother you can talk to? A grandparent? An uncle or aunt? An adult who takes your feelings seriously may be able to challenge your dad and make him see that he needs to take you seriously, too.

Take a break

What if you do all this and your dad is *still* glued to that computer? Let it go for now and try again later. Your dad may be going through a phase that he'll come out of eventually. Or he may be an adult who simply has trouble connecting with kids. Sometimes people like this have better relationships with their children once they've grown. For now, you've done all you can. It's time to stop focusing on your dad and look for love from the members of your family who know how to give it.

living with Dad

I live with my dad. I do not get to see my mom very often. The kids in school talk about their moms. I feel sad. What should I do?

NoMom

Talk to your dad. No one can replace your mom, but if you have a yearning for an older girl or a woman to confide in, he may be able to help you find that kind of friendship. Maybe you can go clothes shopping with your best friend and her mom. Maybe your cousin would go with you to get that new haircut you want. Maybe you and your aunt can go out now and then for tacos and a movie. It'll be fun to have dates where you can talk girl-to-woman about girl sorts of things.

Remember, too, that a first-class dad isn't a second-class parent. You may not have as much of your mom's time as these other girls. But you *do* have a special relationship with a dad who tucks you in at night and helps you with homework and does all sorts of other things with you.

A dad's love

So when other girls are talking about fun things they've done with their moms that week, talk about the fun things you've done with your dad. You're rich in a dad's love and a dad's time. There are probably lots of girls who envy *you* for that.

disappeared dad

My parents divorced when I was five. Now I am twelve. I have not seen my dad for over two years, and I have heard from him only once. Did I do something wrong?

Fatherless

Absolutely not.

When a parent drops out of a child's life, it's because that parent has problems of his or her own. Your father may feel too guilty or too unhappy to visit you. He may not know what to say or do. These are problems he has with his own emotions and actions. They have *nothing* to do with you.

Your father is wrong to be so out of touch. You are a loving, wonderful girl, and he's missing out on sharing the adventure of your growing up. Adults can make mistakes, just as kids do—and this is a huge one.

don't want to go

I see my dad every other weekend and on Wednesdays. His house is a half hour from my house. I hate the drive. Plus I don't have time for my friends, and some of them are dumping me.

LEFT OUT

Feeling left out and spending too much time in a car can be big problems. Yet those Wednesdays and weekends keep you and your dad close. You can't drop them the way you might drop Scouts or viola lessons if your schedule got crazy. The question is how to make the trips better and less upsetting to your social life.

Take friends

Talk to your dad about your friends and see what he suggests. Maybe you can invite a friend—or even a couple of friends—to stay with you at his place now and then.

Flexibility

If your friends have something special planned for a day that you're scheduled to be at your dad's, say so. Ask if you can come a different day or if he and your mom can do the extra driving that will allow you to be included. Your parents might be able to do this or they might not. It doesn't hurt to ask.

Of course, you can't *always* take friends. And you *will* miss some events. Here are some other ways to make the best of it.

Use the time

So here you are, in the car again. Don't sit there looking at road signs and thinking how boring it is. Read a book. Braid a necklace for a friend. Keep busy. It'll occupy your mind, and you'll get out of the car knowing you've accomplished something.

Make it fun

Make this ride a party. Sing. Talk. Tell jokes. Play games. If you don't know any travel games, go online before you leave and find a good one. Have a new game ready for every trip. If it's a long ride, maybe you can go to the same restaurant each time and get a milk shake. Maybe whoever sees the most Canadian license plates gets an extra large.

Stay in touch . . .

But don't overdo it. Between phones and computers you'll have no trouble keeping up with what's going on at home with your friends. That's great. Just don't get so preoccupied with your long-distance conversations that you don't have time to take a walk with your dad.

Get out of the house

There must be all kinds of interesting things going on in your dad's neighborhood that you could be part of. Ask him to help you find a good one. Sign up for the sea sculpture classes at the art center. Learn to do a flip at the local pool. Make the time count.

Make friends

See if you can't make some new friends in your dad's neighborhood, too. You may never feel as close to a weekend friend as you do to your friends at school, but having someone to do things with will make your time at Dad's a whole lot more fun.

Remember

Above all, don't forget what this is all about: your love for your dad and his love for you. The disappointments that come with spending time away from friends can be sharp, but they rarely last long. Dads are forever.

quiz

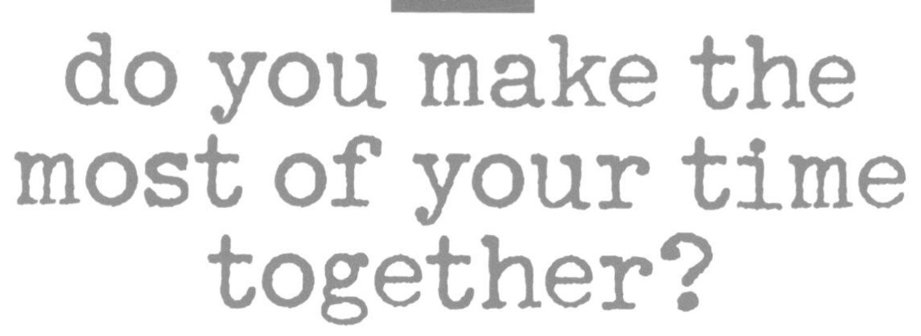

do you make the most of your time together?

Do you ever find yourself in these kinds of situations? Put a check by your answers.

1. You walk in, and the TV is on again. It seems like you never do anything on these weekends with Mom. Oh, well. You throw yourself on the sofa and reach for the remote.

❑ Yes

❑ No

2. You feel so awkward. Dad's new place feels like Mars. Everything looks weird, even the stuff that came from your house. Even Dad.

❑ Yes

❑ No

3. Today Dad bought you everything you asked for at the mall. Tomorrow he's taking you to the arcade and the water park. If you asked for a gold-plated bicycle, he'd probably give you that, too.

❑ Yes

❑ No

4. You're worried all weekend. Is Dad doing O.K.? He looked so sad when you drove off.

☐ **Yes**

☐ **No**

5. *Ohmygosh,* you think. *The soccer tournament is tomorrow.* You'd meant to tell Mom weeks ago. Now you get on the phone and say, "I can't come to see you. I've got soccer." She's upset.

☐ **Yes**

☐ **No**

6. You didn't want to come. From the minute you arrive—sighing and complaining—you let Dad know it.

☐ **Yes**

☐ **No**

7. You're home—tired and crabby and a little sad. Saying good-bye to Dad wasn't easy. Now Mom says, "Quick, put your stuff in your room. We're going to the Murphys'."

☐ **Yes**

☐ **No**

Answers on next page.

answers

If you answered "yes," here's what you need to know:

1. Some adults forget that sitting around watching TV is no way to spend time together. If that situation is familiar, invite your mom or dad to walk to Dairy Queen or kick a soccer ball around the yard. If your parent is pooped? Maybe you can read a book together or play a board game. Don't give in to a couch-potato weekend.

2. A new place can feel funny at first. Don't be afraid to try to make it feel homey for yourself. Turn on the lights. Turn on some music. Put something you love where you can see it. Ask if you and your parent can cook a favorite dinner together. Noise and activity warm a place up.

3. Is it fun when your parents take you places and buy you lots of stuff? Yes. But it may also make you feel funny—as if you're being bribed to forgive them for the divorce or to feel or act a certain way. If you feel weird about being pampered, tell your parent, "I'm happy just being with you. I don't need to have you buy me all these things."

4. Don't worry or feel guilty about the parent you're not with. Your mom and dad are adults. They can take care of themselves.

5. The rules for canceling are the same whether you're a parent or a kid: Don't make it a habit. When you have to cancel, apologize like you mean it. If possible, make plans to be together a little longer next time around.

6. Nothing good can happen if you pack a bad attitude. You're going—that's settled. Being unpleasant about it is only going to annoy your parent—and make you more unhappy than you already are.

7. Saying good-bye can be tough. It's better for a girl to have some quiet time when she goes from one parent to the other. Ask your mom and dad to give you that.

holidays

My parents are in the middle of a divorce. Christmas is coming, and I know things will never be the same. It makes me sad to think about it. Is there any way I can make this Christmas better?

Miserable

Each Christmas carries the memory of all other Christmases. That's what makes holidays wonderful. It's also what makes them hard after a divorce. You can't shut out your memories, and you shouldn't try. You're right to expect some sad moments. When they come over you, let yourself feel what you feel. If you need to cry, do it.

New traditions

Honor your old holiday traditions when you can. When you can't, dream up a couple of activities that might become new traditions. Maybe you can make a gingerbread doghouse on Christmas Eve with your mom. Maybe you can throw a caroling party with your dad and sisters (take pictures!). Maybe it's as simple as stringing popcorn with Mom in front of a holiday video while the baby plays with a cardboard box.

These things may seem small compared with your sadness. But having fun with your family and creating new traditions will remind you that what's most important to you is still here—your parents' love for you, and your love for them. You'll also be planting new memories for Christmases to come. All year they'll grow. Come next year, there they'll be, waiting for you.

advice from girls

Twice the fun

To bring your spirits up about the divorce, think about this: with two homes you get two birthdays, two Christmases, and two family trips!

Grateful

tug-of-war

You love your mom. You love your dad. You want to stay loyal to both. It's easy when they trust and respect each other. It can be a whole lot harder if they disagree a lot. You may feel stuck in the middle—and pulled apart.

Don't despair. There are things you can do to stay out of the family tug-of-war and keep yourself in one piece.

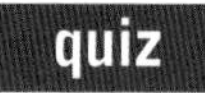

do your parents put you in the middle?

Do one or both of your parents say things like this? Circle each letter where the answer is yes.

a. You want to go on vacation with your father, after all he's done to us? Fine. Leave me here alone.
b. Your father is a loser.
c. Ask your father when he's sending the check. Tell him he's not going to see you till he does.
d. Your father let you see that movie? What's the man thinking?

Answers on next page.

answers

The more circles you made, the more your parents tend to put you in the middle.

a. You have a right to enjoy time with both parents. Neither one should do anything to make you feel bad or guilty about that.

b. Moms and dads simply should not say things like this. To hear one parent bad-mouth the other makes a girl sick at heart the way few other things can.

c. No way should you have to be your parents' messenger. If they have something to say to each other, they should say it directly. Neither one should drag you into discussions about money, and neither should use time with you as a threat.

d. If your mom has problems with your dad's parenting decisions, she should talk to *him*—not you.

e. Prying questions make you feel squirmy. You're not a spy, and nobody should expect you to act like one.

f. Parents sometimes compete with each other without even noticing they're doing it. It makes you feel you have to choose one or the other to love the most. You don't.

g. Parents shouldn't put pressure on you by putting words in your mouth or trying to get you to do something that lands you in a tug-of-war.

h. You should be able to enjoy big days—like holidays, birthdays, graduations, performances, and bat mitzvahs—without worrying. A parent who makes that impossible for you is in the wrong.

Speak up

So what should you do when your mom or dad makes one of these mistakes? Speak up. Say:

Please don't talk like that. It makes me feel terrible.
Please don't put me in the middle. It's not right.
I'm not taking sides. You're wrong to ask me to. I have a right to love both of my parents.

quiz

do you play one parent off the other?

Have you ever said things like this to your parents? Circle each letter where the answer is yes.

answers

When you're full of hurt and anger, there may be times you feel you've got a right to say pretty much anything to your parents to get what you want. You don't. It's wrong for your parents to put you in the middle, and it's just as wrong for you to play one parent off the other.

a. Making your parents feel guilty in order to get something you want is a cheap trick.

b. Don't try to get your dad to fight your battles with your mom (or vice versa). It's a cop-out.

c. Can you make your parents feel more competitive by comparing them? Maybe. Is that good for any of you? No.

d. Using one parent's words to hurt the other destroys trust and respect. It helps create a lousy atmosphere in the family.

e. Take responsibility for your own actions. Don't use your absent parent as an excuse.

f. & g. You may think that being mean will give you revenge for the hurt you've felt. All it really does is make you sad and bitter. Meanness is meanness. It's a bad way to treat other people. It's a bad thing to accept in yourself.

trying to please

Sometimes when I'm supposed to be with my mom, my dad asks me to come to his house. I really don't want to, but I also don't want to hurt his feelings. It's really hard for me to please everyone.

No Name Please

If you don't want to go, don't go. This is a day set aside for you to be with your mom, so there's nothing wrong with saying no to your dad. Be nice and respectful, but tell him, "No, thanks. This is my time with Mom." Your dad's an adult. If he feels disappointed, he can handle it.

Disappointing a parent

You have to learn to handle a parent's disappointment, too. If your dad wants you to do one thing and your mom wants you to do another, they can't both have what they want. If you twist yourself into a pretzel trying to figure out a way to change that, you'll go nuts. A lot of times you just *can't* please everyone. It's impossible.

You're not in charge

You want your parents to be happy. It shows how much you love them. But don't imagine that by being very, very good and doing everything both of them ask you to do you can erase their differences. That's not in your power. Their happiness or unhappiness grows out of how they choose to respond to the joys and difficulties of life. It doesn't depend on whether you say yes or no.

Pleasing yourself

One last thought, and it's a big one: If you worry so much about your parents' feelings that you totally forget about your own, you're going to feel as crushed as a plant growing under a rock. Your feelings are as important as anyone else's. Don't be afraid to express them.

tough stuff

Some emotions may be so strong you think they'll never let go of you. Some situations may make you want to lie down in your tracks and give up.

Don't. Help is there—in your family, at school, in the community. Reach out and get it. If one idea doesn't work, try another. Really tough stuff is not going to be solved overnight. Things may never be perfect, either. But look inside and find the deepest, truest you there is—the you that won't quit. Then go to work with courage and determination. You'll find you're stronger than you think.

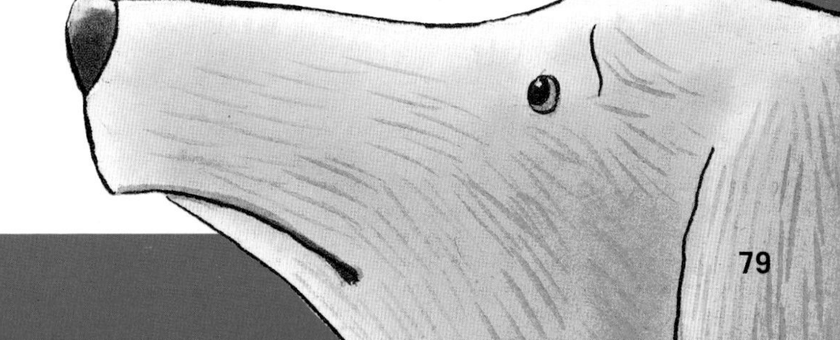

quiz

how are you doing?

Could this be you? Put a check by your answers.

1. Everybody says it's amazing how well you're taking the divorce. Too bad you've been feeling so lousy. Your stomach hurts. Your head aches. Yet you don't have a temperature, and the doctors can't find anything wrong.

❑ **That's me** ❑ **That's not me**

2. You spend hours alone in your room, listening to music and playing a fantasy game you invented. When your dad asks why you don't call a friend, you reply, "I don't feel like it."

❑ **That's me** ❑ **That's not me**

3. Your grades have dropped. You had two detentions this month. Your teacher hates you. You're unpopular. Your life is falling apart.

❑ **That's me** ❑ **That's not me**

4. You used to have a heart, but your parents broke it. Now you spend every hour you can out of the house. Will Dad be moving? Will Mom marry her boyfriend? Whatever. Who cares? Not you.

❑ **That's me** ❑ **That's not me**

5. In your heart of hearts you blame your mom for the divorce, but you would never, ever say so. In fact, for months you've done nothing but help her out and cheer her up.

❑ **That's me** ❑ **That's not me**

answers

1. Miserable feelings can make you sick. Girls who hide their anger and hurt often get headaches, stomach aches, or other pains. To feel better, they need to talk to someone and let those feelings out.

2. A girl full of sadness may feel like closing herself up forever in her room. Don't do it. It's no fun—and no good for your confidence, either. Keep in touch with your friends and stay involved in activities.

3. Trouble at home can lead to trouble at school. If you feel life's a mess, you need to talk to your teacher and a school counselor so that they can help you get back on track.

   Don't pack your problems together, either. They'll take off like a snowball downhill, getting bigger as they go. Instead, think about your problems one by one. In each case, ask yourself, "What can I do about this?" Then do it.

4. Giving up on your family isn't going to make you feel better. It's going to make you sour and lonely. You've been hurt, but don't let that hurt rule your life. Do the truly brave thing and don't cut yourself off from the parents you've always loved.

5. You feel guilty about your feelings and cover them up by being an angel around the house. The problem is that those bad feelings are going to be sitting on a burner in your brain. Talk about your anger now, before it boils over.

Peace

No one can be happy with a war going on in her heart. You need to make peace with your parents' divorce. If you've buried a lot of pain and anger, it's time to dig it up and get rid of it. Step one? Admit you need help and start trying to find it.

money

My mom and dad got divorced. My dad got laid off, and Mom's not making money. The bills are coming out of our ears. That scares me.

Are We Broke?

Money is a problem for many families in the first year or two after a divorce. Parents are earning the same amount as they did before, but they're spending more to run two separate homes. If somebody loses a job or gets laid off, as has happened in your case, parents may worry about money a lot.

Temporary

This situation can be very difficult, but in most families it's temporary. Your parents have earned enough money to pay their bills before. They can do it again. They just need time. Sooner or later your dad will find a new job. If your mom has to, she'll find a job, too. You can earn a little spending money for yourself by babysitting or doing other odd jobs. But trust your parents to straighten out the family finances on their own.

Making choices

In the meantime, don't panic if your mom says something like "We can't afford to get you a new coat this year." It means she's making wise choices. By watching what she spends on small things, she makes sure she can pay for the big ones, like rent and food. She may also know that, however much you want that coat, your old one is warm and you need shoes more.

That can be bad news for a girl who really wants a new coat. But when money's short, accepting the family budget without a scowl is the best help you can give.

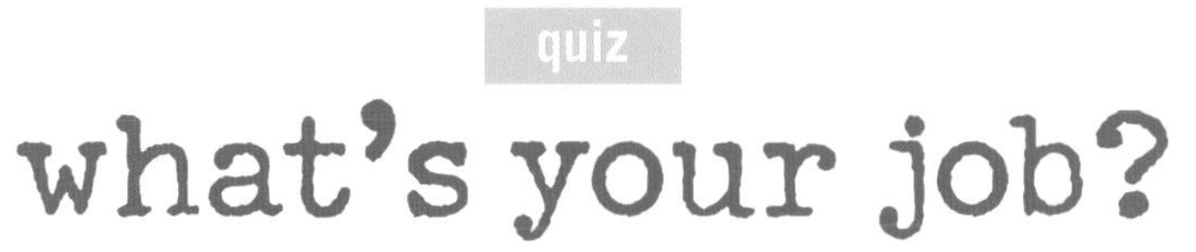

quiz

what's your job?

What should a girl do in situations like these? Put a check by your answers.

1. When Mom went back to work, you became the mom. You're cooking dinner every night—and doing laundry and watching your little brothers. One day you say, "Mom, I'm just a kid. I can't even get my homework done. This is just too much for me."

❑ **Good move** ❑ **Bad move**

2. Dad is really, really depressed. You decide to spend as much time with him as possible to make him happy again.

❑ **Good move** ❑ **Bad move**

3. Your mom is telling you about her date last night. It's O.K. till she gets to the romantic stuff. "Mom," you say, "I'm glad you had a good time, but I don't like talking about this subject."

❑ **Good move** ❑ **Bad move**

4. Jenny asked you to go to the movies, and now Mom wants to come along. It seems like Mom can't be without you for a second. Doesn't she have any friends of her own? You don't want to hurt her feelings, so you say nothing.

❑ **Good move** ❑ **Bad move**

5. Your parents had a big fight on the phone. An hour later, your dad is still upset. "Don't worry, Dad," you say. "We'll be all right. I'll talk to Mom. I'll fix everything."

❑ **Good move** ❑ **Bad move**

answers

1. **Good move**

   Every kid should help out around the house. But if you truly have no time for schoolwork and your own activities, you're carrying a burden too big for a kid. It's good to speak up and say so.

2. **Bad move**

   Depression is a problem that an adult has to fix in his own way, in his own time, with help from other adults. A child simply cannot fix it for him. So you can tell other adults in the family what's going on—maybe they can persuade your dad to see a therapist. But stay involved with your friends and activities. Don't hang around the house and get depressed yourself—don't feel guilty about having fun when your dad's sad, either. He wants you to be happy! Feel free to be so.

3. **Good move**

   You don't need to listen to things that make you uncomfortable.

4. **Bad move**

   It's great for a girl to be close to her parents. It's great for parents and kids to do things together. But if your mom starts playing a big role in your social life, something's wrong. The smart move is to be honest and say, "I was hoping Jenny and I could go alone."

5. **Bad move**

   It's not your job to take care of your mom or dad. For that matter, it's not your job to fill an adult's shoes or carry adult responsibilities. You're a child—not a grownup. Divorce does nothing to change that. Let parents be parents. Don't ever think you have to take charge.

violence

My mom and dad are getting a divorce. My dad is always being mean. He yells, hits, pinches, etc. I'm really scared that my dad is going to hurt me or my mom really bad.

Afraid

It's against the law for your dad to scare and physically hurt you and your mom. This kind of behavior is called domestic abuse. (In your case, the problem is with your dad, but women can commit domestic abuse, too.) Your mother ought to tell the police or a judge what's going on so that the law can protect you. If she hasn't done so, you should. There are people out there who can help.

Call now

Don't wait for the next bad thing to happen. If you have a guardian ad litem or a court counselor, call that person right now. If you don't have a court counselor, talk to a relative. Tell your teacher or a counselor at school. If you get no response, write everything down in a letter and try again. It will show how serious you are. Do anything except keep quiet.

No secrets

Your dad may get angry when he learns you've told. He may also apologize to you and your mom, and promise he'll never, ever hurt you again, provided you change your story and back him up in whatever arguments he makes to the law. Don't listen. *Never keep violence a secret.* Don't spend one single second feeling guilty about telling the truth. Your safety comes first. If he's truly sorry, he'll accept anything that helps him change his terrible behavior.

What then?

When people at court and at school know what your dad is doing, they will use the laws to stop him. Your mom might get an emergency protection order that requires your dad to stay away from you both. If your dad has problems with drugs or alcohol, he may have to enter a treatment program to break these addictions. The court may say that somebody else must be in the room every time he sees you.

If at any time your dad shows up at your house and acts violent, call 911. If you're afraid he'll see you do it, run to a neighbor's and call from there.

the right to feel safe

Every girl has the right to feel safe. That means you shouldn't have to live with fear and violence—whether it's coming from a man or a woman. It also means that no one should touch you in a way that makes you uncomfortable. Anytime anyone violates this right, you have to act. Don't keep secrets. Get help.

dating

Your mom or dad is going on a date with someone new.

It may make you happy. It may make you mad. It may raise a million questions in your mind at a time when you're still getting used to the divorce. But one thing's certain. Dating is never going to change the way your parents feel about you.

normal?

I don't feel comfortable with my parents' dating. I told them how I feel, and they just said it's normal.

Nervous

It *is* normal—for parents to date and for kids to feel a little funny about it at first.

Pink grass

You're used to thinking of your mom and dad as a couple. When you see one of them with someone new, it may feel as if the grass under your feet suddenly turned pink. It just doesn't look right. What's more, you may be embarrassed by seeing your mom or dad acting or talking in a romantic way. You may think: *You aren't a teenager. How can you act so mushy with this person who has nothing to do with us?*

The answer's pretty simple. People like people. If you've ever said "Can I bring a friend?" you know this is true. Enjoying your friend's company doesn't mean you love your family less. It means you and your friend share a lot of interests. Your mom and dad are the same way. They need the friendship of other adults, and when friendship leads to romantic feelings, they date.

Your parents aren't automatically going to marry again simply because they're dating. They're just trying to put the divorce behind them and have some fun. It's a good thing.

Helping you

Try to relax about your parents' dating, and ask them to help by agreeing to these rules:

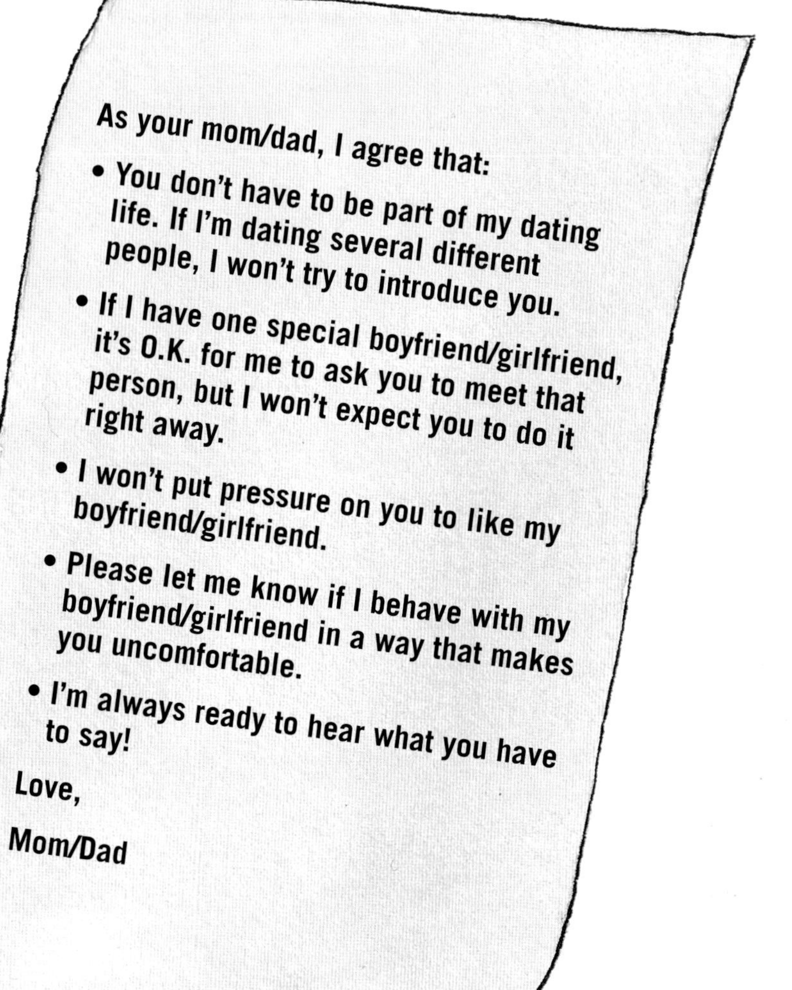

As your mom/dad, I agree that:

- You don't have to be part of my dating life. If I'm dating several different people, I won't try to introduce you.
- If I have one special boyfriend/girlfriend, it's O.K. for me to ask you to meet that person, but I won't expect you to do it right away.
- I won't put pressure on you to like my boyfriend/girlfriend.
- Please let me know if I behave with my boyfriend/girlfriend in a way that makes you uncomfortable.
- I'm always ready to hear what you have to say!

Love,

Mom/Dad

jealous

My dad has a girlfriend. I'm afraid he loves her better than he loves me.

Really Worried

He doesn't love her more

The love a parent feels for a child is different from any other kind of love. You don't have to compete for that love: it's yours—as much a part of you as the nose on your face. It's not going to fade if his love for this girlfriend grows.

Time together

Even kids who know this deep inside might still say, "But those two spend so much *time* together! This person is always with us now. I never get to be alone with my parent anymore."

Less time doesn't mean less love, but it sure can feel that way. A lot of girls grow very close to their parents during a divorce. If a mom or dad suddenly has less time for them, they may feel bitter and abandoned. If that's your story, speak up. Tell your dad, "I know your girlfriend is important to you. But I'm afraid you're not going to love me anymore. Could you and I do one thing a week that's just the two of us together? It will help me feel a lot better."

advice from girls

Sharing

Your parents love you more than anything, and nothing will change that. But you have to realize that your parents want to do fun things just like you do. So if they have a girlfriend or boyfriend, try to be generous and share their time. If you give new people a chance, you might like them.

Keeping an open mind

staying loyal

I'm desperate. My mom's dating my neighbor, but I don't like him. I don't want another dad. I love mine! What would happen if they got married? I swear to the soul I won't accept him.

Daddy's Girl

Accept him as what? A replacement for your dad? It doesn't sound as if anyone's asking you to do that.

Your dad is your dad. Nobody can take his place. Whether your mom marries this neighbor or not, that isn't going to change.

Not an enemy

"Well, maybe," you might say. "But if I talk to this guy and start liking him, it'll hurt my dad's feelings."

It shouldn't. Having a friendly relationship with a guy who makes your mom smile isn't going to make you love your dad less. It isn't going to change the amount of time you spend together or the fun you have.

Don't assume that these two men are enemies, either, battling over your mom. Your parents are divorced. Your mom doesn't have a claim on your dad, and he doesn't have a claim on her. In a lot of cases, parents like yours are *glad* to see each other find new partners and new happiness. You don't have to hate this man to stay loyal to your dad.

Good-bye to wishful thinking

What if you understand all this, but your heart is still saying, *No, no, no*? It may be that, deep down, you've been hoping that your parents would get together again. You hate your mom's friend for getting in the way of your fantasy. If that's the case, you need to ask yourself if your fantasy is getting in the way of real life.

A new relationship

Here's a guy who makes your mom happy—a guy she likes to be with, who laughs at her jokes, who glows when he sees her face. You don't have to accept anything more than that. How your relationship shapes up depends on you both. But don't judge him before you know him. Give him a chance. He deserves it, and so does your mom.

stepparents &

stepfamilies

Moving into the same home doesn't make a family.
But time, patience, and kindness can.

things are fine

My mom has a boyfriend. They're going to get married. I think things are fine with just my mom, my sister, my dog, and me.

Upset

Things *are* fine as they are. Your mom isn't getting married because there's something wrong or because she's unhappy about her life with you. She simply sees no reason to bolt the door against new people and new happiness. She's fallen in love, and it would make her glad to have all the people she loves under one roof.

Talk it over

Tell your mom your fears: *What will it be like, living with this new person? Will we have to move? Will I still spend as much time with Dad? What if you and my stepdad start to argue, and I have to go through another divorce?* Talk it over. Hear what she has to say.

Together, you can make a list of everything in your life that isn't changing. (It'll be a long one.) You should also tell your mom that, after the wedding, you'd like to have a special time alone with her every week. It will help you feel close to her and give you a chance to talk about the divorce, your new stepdad, the news from school, and anything else that's on your mind.

No pressure

If you feel awkward with your stepdad at first, that's natural. You two need time to get to know and trust each other. Be polite and try to get along, but don't put pressure on yourself to feel a certain way. Feeling like a family takes time. So does love. Don't push it. Ask your mom and stepdad not to push it, either.

And remember . . .

Nothing stays the same forever

You can't make life stand still any more than you can nail a wave to the beach. Your mom has made this decision. Take her hand and go with it. Her love for you and your sister is as strong as it ever was. Whatever happens next, you're together—and you can handle it.

advice from girls

Getting used to them

Try to be polite to your stepparent, and a friendly relationship will kick in and flow. Remember, they are getting used to you just as you are to them.

Settled In

her stuff

My stepmother is nice, but she is changing just about our whole house with most of her stuff! I don't like it.

What's Happening Here?

When a parent remarries, ordinary objects may suddenly seem precious. A rug may be loaded with memories. A duck lamp may seem like an expression of who you are. If your stepmom puts them in the basement, you may feel she's out to take over your whole family—past and present.

She's not. When two people marry for the second time, each one brings a homeful of furnishings and a lifetime of habits. It takes a while for everyone to get settled in and adjust to one another. You deserve to be yourself and feel at home. She does, too. You both have to compromise.

Compromise

Tell your dad and stepmom you wish more of your old stuff could stay. Maybe your stepmom doesn't want the rug back in the kitchen, but she'd be glad to put it in the hall. Maybe the duck lamp would look great on your desk. Ask for control of your own room, too. It will be easier to see all the changes in the living room if you know there's a place where you can do what you like.

Finally, make a list of all the good things that came in the door with this nice stepmom—not just the Ping-Pong table, but the bike rides and the laughter, too. Don't forget them.

his name

> I have a stepdad. He wants me to call him Dad. But I just can't. He annoys me every day with the same remark: "Don't call me Doug. Call me Dad."
>
> *Annoyed*

You don't have to call him Dad if you don't want to.
Tell your stepdad, "I'm not comfortable calling you Dad. If you don't want me to call you Doug, let's come up with a nickname together." Maybe his parents have always called him by a special name that you could use, too.

"Please stop"
Your stepdad won't compromise and keeps saying the same old thing, then he may not understand how hurtful it is to put pressure on kids about the names Mom and Dad. Ask your mom to explain it to him. You can tell him, too:

bonkers

I don't know what's wrong with me, but my stepfather drives me bonkers. When my mom asks me to do the same thing he's asked me, I don't go bonkers. I just say "O.K., Mom."

Hothead

Nothing's wrong with you. You're just trying to get used to having your stepdad tell you what to do. It's one of the hardest things in a new stepfamily. Teachers, babysitters, other moms and dads—a girl listens to lots of adults. But stepparents stir up your feelings. A voice inside growls, *You're not my real dad!* even though you know that this has nothing to do with whether or not you should pick up your socks.

Family rules

Think of it this way: Being a member of a family comes with certain responsibilities and expectations. Who does which chores? What manners should you use? Can you eat in the living room or not? In a new stepfamily, people may have different ideas about how to answer these sorts of questions. It helps if the whole family sits down and talks about this stuff. What's expected? What's allowed? Agree on the family rules. It will be easier for you to hear your stepdad say "Set the table" if you and your mom have already agreed that it's your job to do it.

Parenting rules

There are other kinds of rules that grow from parenting decisions: "That dress is too short. Don't wear it." "I expect you to get better grades." "You can't see PG-13 movies." These parenting rules should come from your mom. She may ask your stepdad to help her *enforce* them, but he's not in charge of you in the same way. It may make you relax to talk to your mom now and then and be reminded of that.

Keep talking

Right now, your new family is like a puzzle you're all working on together. How do the pieces fit? What role does everyone play? That may be as hard for your stepdad to figure out as it is for you. As you two get used to each other, the pieces will fall into place. You'll go bonkers less often. In time, you may trust and understand him in a deeper way. And that will make rules and just about everything else in this relationship a lot easier.

advice from girls

Looking out for you

Sometimes it's hard to have a stepparent because it is another person to make rules and another person to listen to. But it also means more people to look out for you and more people to love you.

Feeling Loved

wicked stepparent?

My mom married someone I hate. He's been with us for about two years. I can't stand him.

Depressed

Where's this hate coming from? That's the question you have to ask yourself—and answer honestly.

Mistreatment?

If you hate your stepdad because he mistreats you, talk to your mom. Mistreatment includes hitting, threats, name-calling, outright cruelty, and the kind of touching you know is wrong. If your mom doesn't do anything about it, talk to someone else in your family. Talk to a counselor at school or someone at court. No one should have to live with behavior like this, and you've got every right in the world to get help to stop it.

Disagreements?

If you hate your stepdad because you disagree a lot, it may be that you two don't understand or sympathize with each other because he wasn't around when you were growing up. This can be hard, but it's not hopeless.

Pick three things that bug you about the relationship. Come up with a plan to cool down the fights. Get a third person involved. Maybe your mom can lay down some rules for a truce. Maybe a family therapist could help. All this may not make you love your stepdad, or even like him. But it *will* help the two of you live in the same house.

Stubbornness?

If you hate your stepdad because you just never wanted your mom to get married in the first place, it's time to ask yourself if hate should be such a big part of your life.

Hate can cloud your eyes and plug your ears. Everything your stepdad does may look bad. Everything he says may seem mean. You may see a creep when there's a perfectly O.K. guy at the dinner table trying to get along.

If this is your story, you need to end the war you declared back when your mom decided to marry. Maybe you wouldn't have picked this man, but your mom did. It was her choice to make. Your stepdad isn't perfect, but neither are you. It's time to climb out of your trench and lay down your hatred. Try peace. It's a whole lot lighter on the spirit.

advice from girls

Being nice

My dad remarried last year. It was real hard on me. I hated my stepmother. I wanted to make her unhappy and make her wish she hadn't married my dad. But she was really nice to me. I began to like her. I found out it was easier being nice to her than being mean.

Feeling Better

the third sister

My mom is marrying her boyfriend. He has two daughters. They're really excited about getting a third sister. But they're used to having a sister. I'm not.

Worried

Talk to friends who have brothers and sisters. Chances are, they'll say that there are things they like about it and things they don't. That's likely to be true for you, too.

The difference is that you and these two girls won't have grown up together. No one should expect you to feel like sisters right away. Love doesn't show up at the door with the mail. It has to grow. It will take time for everyone to get to know one another. Just be patient and do your best to get along. Trust and affection will follow in their own time. Here's what to expect along the way:

Three people

Your stepsisters and stepdad are three different people. You'll have a unique relationship with each one—which will change as you go along.

Jealousy

It can be hard to share a parent with other kids, especially if they get to see your parent more than you do. You may get angry with these girls for "hogging" your mom's time, and worry that she'll come to love them more than she does you.

No way. If your mom had a hundred daughters to love and care for, it wouldn't change the way she feels about you. Confide your fears, let her reassure you, and ask for some time alone with her every week.

Compromises

You'll have to share more now. You'll have to wait your turn and won't always get first pick. Just remind yourself that you girls are all in this together. Your stepsisters are making compromises for you, too.

Differences

You and your stepsisters may like to watch different shows, wear different clothes, spend time with different sorts of people. Make up your mind right now that differences are O.K. You all need to accept one another for who you are.

Fights

Now and then, you and your stepsisters will fight. All sisters do—even those who've grown up together. Talk it over once you've calmed down, and everything will be fine. If you have trouble making up? Have a family meeting. Five heads may be better—and cooler—than two.

Quiet time

Give yourself some quiet time every day. Curl up with a book. Sit in the grass and pet the cat. In a big family, it helps to stop now and then to take a breather and think your own thoughts. Ask your sisters to respect your privacy during this time, and do the same for them when they need to be alone.

Fun

While you're at it, don't forget to enjoy all the good things about having this new family. You three girls can help one another with your homework, tell riddles in the backseat of the car, stand up for one another at school. You can share stuff—clothes, music, scrunchies, computer games, books. Three kids means more to talk about at dinner—and more help cleaning up afterward. There may be more spats in the house, but there could well be more laughter, too. Best of all, you're going to have more people to care for—and more people to care for you.

boring house

My dad just got married again. I love my new family so much that I want to go live with them. My mom is who I live with now, but I have nothing to do here. There's plenty to do there.

Bored

If you can arrange with your parents to spend a bit more time at your dad's, that's great. But moving in right now would be a mistake. There are a lot of changes going on in your family. Everyone—including you—needs to let things settle down before making more.

One big party?

Have you heard the saying "The grass is always greener on the other side of the fence"? It means that people tend to want what they don't have. If you've seen your dad and new stepfamily on weekends and vacations, you may picture your life with them as one big party. But if you lived there full-time, daily life would probably include the same chores and annoyances—and boring moments—that you complain about at your mom's. You don't want to get so carried away with your enthusiasm for your dad's house that you forget what's always been wonderful about your mom's.

The truth is, there are good reasons for wanting a change in custody, but being bored isn't one of them. The question of where you should live is a whole lot bigger and more complicated than that.

grabby kids

My mom just got remarried, and now there are three little kids in the family. All they do is ruin my things. My mom said to put the things that are important to me away. But they just find them again.

Crazed

Your mom's suggestion is a good one. Maybe you just need to put your things in a better place.

Box it, lift it, lock it

Stick your special stuff in boxes. With a lot of little kids, out of sight is out of mind. Put the boxes up high, where they're hard to notice and harder to get to. Go to a discount store and buy a simple metal lockbox. Lockboxes don't cost much, and they give you a great place to stash smaller things, like your diary.

If you're going to your dad's for a while, ask your mom if you can stick a box in her closet. Maybe your glass hippopotamus can live in the china cabinet till these kids get older and less grabby—which they will.

new baby

My mom got remarried, and now they're having a baby. They're buying all this new stuff, and when I talk to them, sometimes they don't even listen and keep on talking about the baby. What should I do?

Feeling Lost

Babies arrive in a blizzard of excitement. It's not uncommon for a girl to feel buried and forgotten in all the fuss. If this baby is coming after a divorce and remarriage, as it is in your case, a voice may crop up in the back of your brain saying, *Mom loves the baby's dad more than my dad. Does that mean she'll love the baby more than me?*

The only you

Not a chance. That baby will be loved and cherished, but you are the only you there is. Not one atom of you is replaceable. You have a place in your mom's heart that nothing and nobody can touch. If you don't believe it, ask her. She'll be more than happy to take you in her arms and set you straight.

Join the team

You should also talk about what to expect once the baby comes home. Babies take up lots of their parents' time and attention. You aren't going to feel good about it till you stop thinking of the baby as something your mom and stepdad are doing without you and start thinking of the baby as something you're all doing together.

Ask your mom how you can be included. Can you help set up the baby's room? Can you help pick out the crib? Can you dust off that old stroller that's been sitting in the basement? Learn a few lullabies and nursery rhymes. Get psyched.

When the baby comes home, your mom will have more chores and less sleep. Here again, pitching in may be the best way not to feel left out. While your mom feeds the baby, fold the laundry and tell her about gymnastics. Rock the baby while she cooks dinner and gives you advice on your science project. Bring in the paper. Change a diaper. She'll be glad for the help, and you'll be glad for the time together.

Be a sister

Finally, remember that night feedings and dirty diapers aren't going to last forever. This baby is going to grow up fast. Before you know it, he or she is going to be standing on two feet, checking out the world. This little person is going to look up to you in a special way. Enjoy it. Be warm. Be funny. Be loving. Don't hold back. After all, this is your family, too.

more advice from girls

Not the only one
My parents have been divorced for six years. At first you think you're the only one that it is happening to, but you're not. Other people have the same problem. It helps to say this in your mind.

A Girl Like You

There for you
Remember that both your parents still love you dearly. If you need them, they'll always be there for you, even if they're not together.

Loved

Getting over it
When my parents divorced, I was mad for a long time. But I got over it. Now some people ask me, "Do you hate your parents?" I say, "No. Why should I? It was their choice. They didn't have the same feeling for each other."

Not a Hater

The long run

Often mothers and fathers are better, happier parents when they're apart. It's tough at first, but in the long run you'll like your parents a lot more.

Survivor

Better off

My parents divorced four years ago. It felt strange not having both parents in the house. For a long time, I was really sad and wished they would get back together. But eventually I realized it was better this way. There isn't fighting all the time. Everybody is better off. My mom is happier, my dad is happier, and I'm really happier, too.

Better Now

Talking

What helped me was counseling, my family, and friends. I would suggest talking to good friends and family. You would be surprised at how supportive they can be.

Found Help

It takes time

When my mom remarried, my older brother and sister tried to pick fights to get our stepdad to leave. Or they would try to make my mom choose between them. When they realized it wasn't working, they stopped. I think knowing that our stepdad isn't leaving us makes us all feel safe. I guess it just takes time.

Learning

Things in common

I get along with my stepmother because I know she is not taking my mother's place in life. We like to share things we have in common. For example, we both love my father.

Sharing Dad

Support each other

My dad just got remarried. I felt terrible at first. I was crying and crying. But I cheered up because my father is really happy. He went through a divorce and supports me and works. So I feel I should give him some support.

Loyal Daughter

Feeling secure

My mom, sister, and I lived alone for a while. When my stepdad came along, I felt more secure. My dad lives about an hour and a half away. It took a while for me to get used to my stepdad, but I realized after about two years that he's there for me when my real dad can't be.

Glad for Stepdad

Give it a chance

When my mom remarried, I hated it. I didn't like having a stepdad, brother, or sister. Then I realized things weren't going to change. So I gave things a chance, and it wasn't so bad after all. I'm really lucky to have a family who loves me, and who I love.

Surprised

Getting along

It's important to build a friendship with everyone in your new family. If something about one person annoys you or makes you mad, try and find things about her you appreciate, respect, or have in common. You'll find you get along better.

Trying My Best

And finally . . .

Here's a **Girl's Bill of Rights** that sums up much of what you've read in this book. Get out the scissors and cut along the dotted line on the opposite page. Post your Girl's Bill of Rights on the refrigerator, or the bathroom mirror, or the bulletin board in your room. Look at it before you march out the door in the morning. Look at it again before you climb into bed at night. Make the ideas your own, and feel confident doing it.

a girl's bill of rights

1. I have a right to feel the way I feel about my parents' divorce.

2. I have a right to say what I think and speak up when things are bothering me.

3. I have a right to ask questions and get answers about our family's future.

4. I have a right not to feel guilty about the divorce.

5. I have a right to have a continuing relationship with both of my parents.

6. I have a right not to take sides. I'm free to be loyal and loving to both my parents.

7. I have a right not to hear my parents say bad things about each other.

8. I have a right to say no to a parent who tries to use me as a messenger or a spy or who gets me involved in disagreements about money.

9. I have a right to feel safe.

10. I have a right to celebrate big days and holidays without worrying.

11. I have a right to find help if I need it.

12. I have a right to be proud of my family and to look forward to a happy future.

Here are some other American Girl books you might like:

❑ I read it.

❑ I read it.

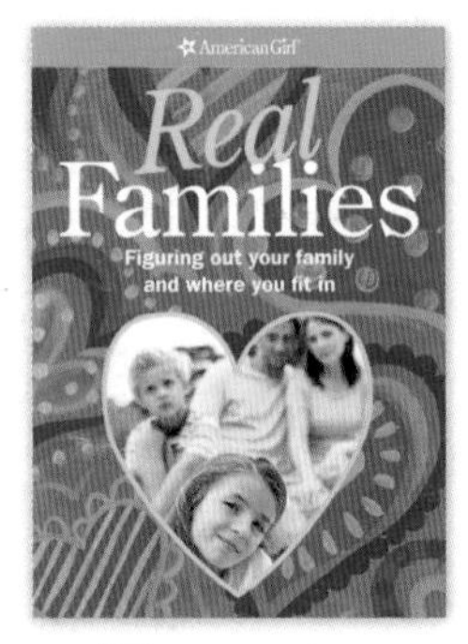

❑ I read it.

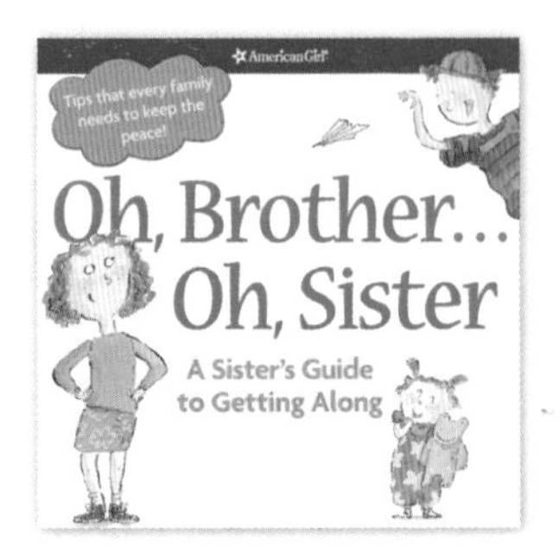

❑ I read it.

❑ I read it.

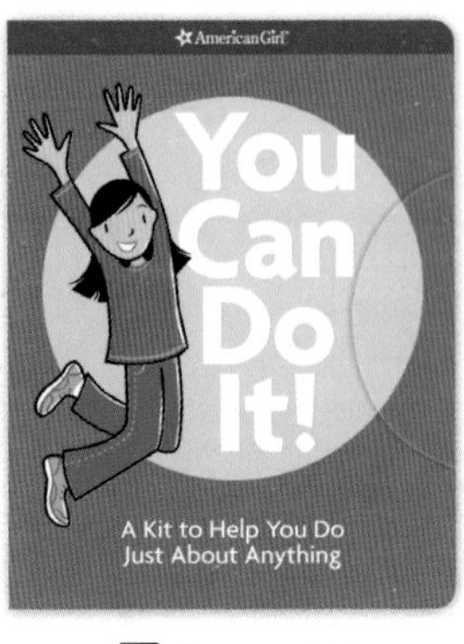

❑ I read it.